Rewriting Life's Rules

How to Break Free from Society

Danielle Lee

Copyright © 2025 by Danielle Lee
Published by: Hille House Publishing

ISBN: 978-1-7641985-6-1 (Paperback)
ISBN: 978-1-7641985-7-8 (E-book)

Disclaimer

The author of this book does not dispense medical advice or prescribe the use of any technique as a form of treatment for physical, emotional, or medical problems, either directly or indirectly, without the advice of a physician. The intent of the author is only to offer information of a general nature to help you on your quest for emotional, mental and spiritual support on your personal journey. In the event the readers use any of the information in this book for themselves, the author and publisher assume no responsibility for their actions.

All Rights Reserved

Apart from any fair dealing for the purpose of research or private study, criticism, or review, as permitted under the Copyright, Designs, and Patents Act 1988, this publication may only be reproduced, stored, or transmitted in any form or by any means with the prior permission in writing of the copyright owner, or in the case of the reprographic reproduction, in accordance with the terms of licensees issued by the Copyright Licensing Agency. Enquiries concerning reproduction outside those terms should be sent to the author at www.lovinglyguided.com

Contents

Acknowledgments	V
Introduction	VII
How This Book Works	
1. What Are Beliefs and Rules, and How They Shape Our Reality	1
2. How Beliefs are Formed	15
3. Rewriting your Beliefs and Rules	25
4. Love Learning Self-Love, Unconditional Love, and Love within Relationships	37
5. Relationships Rewriting the Rules of Connection	57

6. Money   71
Rewriting the Rules to Let Abundance Flow In

7. Business and Success   83
Defining It for Ourselves

8. Time   97
Rewriting Our Rules to Get Time Back

9. Reclaiming Your Worth   119
You Were Always Enough

10. Epilogue   141

11. About the Author   143

Acknowledgments

This book would be nothing without the help from my beautiful Mowmow. You inspire me each and every day.

Also Thank you, Cameron and Jonny, for showing me that I can live a "limitless life."

And thank you, Mandy Morris, for showing me what true unconditional love really looked like, especially when I needed it the most.

Introduction

How This Book Works

Do you ever just sit there and think, *How did I get here? This isn't the life I imagined for myself. I thought I'd be happier by now. Is this really all there is?*

If you've ever felt that way, trust me—you're not alone. Those thoughts ran through my mind for years, leaving me stuck, restless, and unsure how to break free. I felt lost and didn't even realize I had the power to change things—that I could actually rewrite my story. It took hitting rock bottom for me to finally see the truth: I was in control. The only thing that needed to shift were the beliefs and rules I had been living by.

So many of us are walking through life carrying beliefs we didn't choose—beliefs shaped by childhood, trauma, culture, or fear. But what if we could question those beliefs? What if we could choose again?

Around that time, my mom introduced me to Mandy Morris, the co-founder of Authentic Living. Mandy runs a program focused on personal growth and healing and has written several books. When I first heard about her, she had just released a new book, *The 8 Secrets to Manifestation*, and was offering a free 8-day live event to those who pre-ordered it. My mom bought me a copy, and I joined the event.

Toward the end of that experience, Mandy spoke about her coaching certification program. I sat with the idea for a few days… and then I decided to go for it. While going through the course, the concept of *rewriting your rules* came up again. I asked, "How do you rewrite them in a way your subconscious actually believes?" She answered, "Rewrite them in a way your subconscious can accept."

That line stuck with me. I had to sit with it for a while before it really clicked—but when it did, everything changed. And that's when the idea for this book was born.

Rewriting your rules means identifying the hidden beliefs that have been shaping your life—and consciously choosing new ones that align with who you really are and the life you want to create. It's not just mindset work—it's soul work.

This was one of the hardest lessons I've ever had to learn—but also the most life-changing. Once I embraced it, new opportunities started to unfold. My life began to transform in ways I never thought possible.

This book is a guide for anyone who's ever felt stuck, disconnected, or like they're living by someone else's rules. Inside, you'll learn how to break free from outdated beliefs, reconnect with your truth, and create a life that feels like *yours*. I'll share my own experiences with you—honestly and openly—as we walk through the core areas of life and how I personally redefined them.

Together, we'll break down the rules that once held you back, and I'll walk you through the process of rewriting the ones that will move you forward. Each of us is the author of our own story. And for your story to feel aligned, each area of your life deserves to be balanced and connected in a way that feels true to *you*.

You've followed the old rules long enough. Now, it's time to remember: you are the creator of your life. Let's make it a beautiful one.

What Are Beliefs and Rules, and How They Shape Our Reality

We all live by a set of beliefs and rules—some we consciously choose, others we've absorbed without even realizing it. These unseen frameworks quietly shape how we think, behave, and make sense of the world. They influence what we strive for, how we respond to challenges, and even what we believe we deserve. But where do these beliefs come from? And what happens when they no longer serve us? To understand how deeply they shape our lives, we first need to look at what they actually are.

Let's start with the simple definitions of both *beliefs* and *rules*. According to the Merriam-Webster Dictionary, *belief* is defined as:

- A state or habit of mind in which trust or confidence is placed in some person or thing

- Something that is accepted, considered to be true, or held as an opinion

- Conviction of the truth of some statement or the reality of some being or phenomenon, especially when based on examination of evidence

And *rule* is defined as:

- A prescribed guide for conduct or action

- The laws or regulations prescribed by the founder of a religious order for observance by its members

- An accepted procedure, custom, or habit

Even these simple definitions reveal how powerful beliefs and rules can be in shaping our lives. We develop them based on our personal experiences, social and cultural conditioning, and emotional and psychological factors. Over time, they become the invisible boundaries of our world—often guiding us long after we've forgotten where they came from.

Snapshot of My Life

I grew up in an affluent area where most families were upper-middle class or above. It was the kind of place where people didn't lock their doors or worry about their cars being broken into. Life felt safe, protected, and insulated—a bubble that convinced me the world was supposed to work that way. That illusion shattered during the 2008 economic crash. My bubble popped, and I realized life didn't always follow the rules I'd been taught.

That crash was a major turning point in my life. It forced me to start forming new beliefs—especially around money and stability. Like many teens, I had a rocky relationship with my father. Most of our conflicts centered on how I wanted to live versus how he thought I should. After my parents divorced when I was fifteen, my brother and I moved in with him. Though I didn't show it at the time, it affected me deeply.

I began forming unconscious rules about relationships, how they were "supposed" to work and how love was shown. Around that time, I also began struggling with depression, though I didn't recognize it for what it was. I assumed there was something inherently wrong with me. I later realized my first suicidal thoughts had started around age six, and they only intensified as I got older.

In my senior year of high school, I pushed myself hard. I took three Advanced Placement classes and an early-morning college course through a dual enrollment program. If I passed everything, I would've completed my first semester of college before even setting foot on campus. Looking back, I realize I was trying to prove something to myself and to everyone else that I was smart enough to succeed.

When I moved to North Carolina in first grade, I was the only student in my class who couldn't read yet. It was devastating. I was teased relentlessly, and the wounds from that time stayed with me. For years, I struggled with spelling, and one teacher even recommended I repeat a grade. They suspected I had dyslexia or ADHD, but my mom refused to put me on medication—something I'm grateful for now. Still, I felt like I had to work twice as hard just to keep up. This insecurity only grew when my younger brother seemed to absorb information effortlessly. I took it as proof that something was wrong with me.

As college approached, the fear of failure became overwhelming. I was terrified I wouldn't be able to handle the academic pressure. At the same time, I was deeply passionate about marine biology and coral reef conservation. I dreamed of living on an island, teaching scuba diving, and protecting the ocean. But when I shared that dream, it sparked a huge argument with my dad. He told me I'd be setting myself up for failure if I didn't go to college. So, I compromised; I chose a marine biology program at an out-of-state school where I knew no one from my high school would be.

I don't regret going to college. I met incredible people, many of whom are still in my life. I participated in fascinating research and learned a great deal, despite the challenging coursework. But I carried the mindset of "Cs get degrees," which led to procrastination, not putting in the study time I needed for passing grades and many missed opportunities for deeper growth. All because I wasn't willing to miss out on a good party.

After graduating early, I was shocked by how hard it was to find a job. I assumed it would be easy, but most positions required a master's degree and prior experience, usually gained through unpaid internships. I was lost and unsure how I'd make ends meet. That's when I joined the Coast Guard, a decision many of my college friends mocked, saying, "You only joined because you couldn't find a real job."

Let me be clear: I will always be proud of and thankful for the men and women who choose to serve regardless of their reasons. It's not easy, and most people have no idea the sacrifices involved in protecting our country.

Basic training was one of the hardest things I've ever done physically and mentally. It's designed to break you down and rebuild you. You're forced to adopt new rules quickly, many of which didn't align with who I was at my core.

People often ask if I regret joining. My answer is always no. I loved every job I had during active duty. The Coast Guard took me places I never thought I'd go, including California, a lifelong dream of mine. I met incredible people and had unforgettable experiences, but I also endured some of the hardest moments of my life. Both the highs and lows shaped who I am today.

I met my ex-husband while stationed in Bahrain, although we didn't become close until we both ended up in California. He was attending his "A" school while I was stationed in San Francisco. We were part of a close-knit group that spent every weekend together, often crashing at my apartment. We partied hard, and I was completely unaware of how quickly my life was spiraling.

He and I would stay up late having deep conversations, and I remember thinking, *Wow, he's like the male version of me.* What I didn't realize at the time was that he was mirroring me, feeding me the exact words I wanted to hear.

After our group graduated, loneliness crept in. When I needed a plus-one for a family wedding, he came with me. That's when we came up with the idea to get married. The plan was to avoid being stationed apart, try dating, and if it didn't work out, just stay friends. I thought it was the perfect plan with no risk involved. Looking back, I have no idea why I thought that was a good plan. The only explanation I can offer is that I was deeply lonely, yet terrified of real commitment. I didn't believe I deserved genuine love, especially after I'd hurt an amazing person in a previous relationship.

In the beginning, it felt like a fairytale. I was in the middle of a love-bombing phase, getting all the attention I'd craved for years. But over time, things started to shift subtly at first. I blamed the changes on stress, lack of sleep, depression, and the grief I felt after losing my dog. I had relied on that dog for comfort and safety more than I realized.

During college, I had experienced a traumatic event where a man repeatedly broke into my apartment. One night, I woke up to find him standing over me. It left a scar both physically and emotionally. I never told anyone and carried that trauma for years. When I finally sought help, the doctor immediately prescribed depression medication without taking the time to understand my history. The side effects overwhelmed me, and within a month, I was in an inpatient program.

But my true rock bottom came when I checked into that same inpatient facility for the second time in the same year, only a few years ago. My relationship had become toxic and abusive. I was living in a constant state of fight or flight. I couldn't sleep, barely ate, and felt completely numb. I was so overmedicated that I couldn't feel anything, becoming a shell of myself, wandering through life in a fog.

Then something shifted. The relationship ended. I was devastated at first and begged him not to leave. But he told me the only way he knew how to punish me was to separate for a while. The night before, I had started another fight—part of a pattern I couldn't seem to stop. Now I understand that when we're in an abusive relationship, we begin reacting in automatic ways. It's our subconscious trying to protect us, signaling that something is deeply wrong. Those reactions were attempts to break free from a trauma bond I didn't yet recognize.

Looking back, I also suspect that he wanted space because he was about to leave for college in

Charleston. He had always been jealous of the freedom I once had, and later, I found out there were other girls involved. A few days after the breakup, I reached out, asking what I could do to fix things. He told me I needed to focus on myself, heal, and overcome my codependency. In hindsight, that was the best thing he could have said.

Despite everything, I'm grateful to him. That relationship became the catalyst I needed to begin healing from past trauma.

Four months after our separation, I started to feel like myself again. I began enjoying life more, staying present, and appreciating everyday moments. But eventually, I hit a plateau in therapy. It felt like we were going in circles, revisiting the same wounds. I was ready to grow beyond them.

I adored my therapist—she helped me more than she probably knows. But I needed something different, something more forward-focused. That's when I decided to hire my first life coach.

It was a huge and uncomfortable step. I had never invested so much in myself before, spending $3,000 on a 90-day program. But I was willing to try anything, and it was worth every penny. It was the first real investment I made in *myself, and* I know I'll work with her again someday.

She helped me build self-confidence, taught me how to keep promises to myself, and encouraged me to get back out into the world. I began going out more, enjoying solo activities, and learning how to truly be okay alone. I took myself on dinner dates, went dancing, snowboarding, and even camping—all on my own. I realized I could explore and create meaningful experiences without needing anyone else to be there.

Now, I genuinely crave solitude—in a healthy way. But the most important thing she taught me was this: *I am in control of my life. I have the power to write my own story.*

Charleston. He had always been jealous of the freedom I once had, and later, I found out there were other girls involved. A few days after the breakup, I reached out, asking what I could do to fix things. He told me I needed to focus on myself, heal, and overcome my codependency. In hindsight, that was the best thing he could have said.

Despite everything, I'm grateful to him. That relationship became the catalyst I needed to begin healing from past trauma.

Four months after our separation, I started to feel like myself again. I began enjoying life more, staying present, and appreciating everyday moments. But eventually, I hit a plateau in therapy. It felt like we were going in circles, revisiting the same wounds. I was ready to grow beyond them.

I adored my therapist—she helped me more than she probably knows. But I needed something different, something more forward-focused. That's when I decided to hire my first life coach.

It was a huge and uncomfortable step. I had never invested so much in myself before, spending $3,000 on a 90-day program. But I was willing to try anything, and it was worth every penny. It was the first real investment I made in *myself, and* I know I'll work with her again someday.

She helped me build self-confidence, taught me how to keep promises to myself, and encouraged me to get back out into the world. I began going out more, enjoying solo activities, and learning how to truly be okay alone. I took myself on dinner dates, went dancing, snowboarding, and even camping—all on my own. I realized I could explore and create meaningful experiences without needing anyone else to be there.

Now, I genuinely crave solitude—in a healthy way. But the most important thing she taught me was this: *I am in control of my life. I have the power to write my own story.*

At the time, this was a foreign concept to me. For so long, I believed the life I dreamed of wasn't possible. I thought I had to follow the traditional path: 9-to-5 job, limited vacation, constant burnout. But what if I could travel the world, work fewer hours, make more money, and be genuinely happy?

It was exhilarating and terrifying. I knew exactly what kind of life I wanted, but my mind constantly resisted. I sabotaged myself over and over again. Still, I learned enough to know that I wanted to help others. If I could find my light again, I could help others find theirs, too.

I don't regret anything, none of the pain, mistakes, or dark chapters. Every experience shaped the person I am today, and I love who I've become. My hope is that through your own journey of rewriting your beliefs, you also take a moment to honor how far you've come and embrace who you are becoming.

How Beliefs are Formed

As humans, we are not meant to live in isolation; we are deeply connected to the societies and cultures that shape us. From the moment we are born, we're influenced by the beliefs and values instilled in us by our families, communities, and cultures. These beliefs often become the foundation for how we navigate the world. Over time, we create rules around them to ensure they remain intact.

However, many of the beliefs we adopt can be limiting, preventing us from fully realizing our potential and becoming our true, authentic selves.

Every culture carries its own set of ideas about what is considered acceptable, valuable, and "normal." These cultural norms influence how we perceive success, beauty, happiness, family roles, and even spirituality. For instance, in many Western cultures, individual hard work is highly praised, and people are often judged by their achievements. In contrast, Eastern cultures tend to emphasize family and community, with personal goals taking a backseat to collective well-being.

I've traveled to many countries, and one thing I've noticed is that while Western cultures often "live to work," Eastern cultures typically "work to live."

Religious beliefs also play a significant role in shaping our worldview. Consider someone raised Christian versus someone raised Jewish. One might celebrate Christmas, the other Hanukkah. These traditions shape their identities and understanding of the world. I don't believe there's a singular "correct" religion or belief system; it's more about what resonates with us and what we choose to carry forward in our lives.

Within our cultures, families pass down their own sets of beliefs from generation to generation beliefs that can be difficult to challenge. I grew up in a family that believed the key to success was attending college. But imagine you have a deep yearning to live on a tropical island and work on a snorkeling charter boat all year-round. Your heart longs for a simple, adventurous life, but your subconscious tells you, *That's not possible.*

Many of us have been taught that success requires a traditional career path, college followed by a stable corporate job. So, we follow that path, even when it doesn't align with our true desires. Eventually, we might find ourselves working in a job unrelated to our degree, still searching for fulfillment. Why? Because we believed our only option was to go to college and ignore our dream.

These generational beliefs often go unquestioned because they are passed down with love, care, and the best of intentions. But as we grow older and are exposed to new experiences and perspectives, those long-held beliefs can start to feel restrictive or outdated.

In today's world, the media plays a powerful role in shaping our beliefs. It presents idealized versions of how life should look, what success is, what happiness feels like, and what we should aspire to become.

Social media, in particular, has become a dominant influence. We are constantly bombarded with curated snapshots of other people's lives, their careers, relationships, and appearances and it's easy to fall into the trap of thinking our own lives are lacking in comparison. We begin to believe that life must look a certain way to be valuable or meaningful, which causes us to operate from a mindset of lack.

Think about how popular true crime content has become everywhere. I don't know many people who *don't* watch it. But by consistently consuming this type of media, it can start to affect how we view the world. Our beliefs shape our perceptions, and the content we consume reinforces those beliefs.

For example, if you constantly watch true crime and murder mysteries, you may begin to perceive the world as dangerous and unsafe. Your brain will naturally search for evidence to support that belief, heightening your sense of fear and anxiety. I experienced this personally and eventually chose to stop watching those shows. As a result, I began to feel more at ease in my daily life.

That said, it's still important to listen to our intuition and practice caution when necessary. But I no longer walk around expecting something bad to happen at every corner. This shift in mindset has allowed me to travel solo with more trust in others, and I've had nothing but positive experiences.

For instance, during a month-long stay in Costa Rica, I regularly encountered a homeless man each morning. He was always kind and never gave off a threatening vibe. Over time, we exchanged casual conversations, and I got to know him. In the past, I might have avoided him out of fear, but now I see that people are often misunderstood, and kindness can be found everywhere.

It's easy to get caught up in the negative narratives portrayed in the media. If we only consume information from one biased source, our worldview becomes increasingly narrow.

I remember when I traveled to Brazil for a friend's wedding. My parents were anxious because they'd heard it was unsafe. But when I arrived in the small beach town, I felt welcomed and secure. Despite the language barrier, people were kind and generous. By the end of the trip, I knew most of the locals who worked at the restaurants and bars. The media doesn't tell the whole story.

Similarly, when I lived in Bahrain, I was trained on the potential risks of the region before moving there.

While there are certainly unsafe areas in the Middle East, as in any part of the world, the culture was overwhelmingly welcoming and friendly. I actually felt safer there than in many places in the U.S.

These experiences showed me how easy it is to form beliefs based on what we're told rather than what we personally experience.

Our environment is one of the most powerful forces shaping our beliefs and behaviors often more than we realize. The people we surround ourselves with, the conversations we engage in, and the energy of the places we live all influence how we think and what we believe is possible.

You've probably heard the saying, "You are the average of the five people you spend the most time with." There's truth to that. When we spend time around people who are constantly negative or limited by fear, it becomes easy to mirror that mindset. Likewise, when we surround ourselves with people who dream big, take risks, and operate from abundance, it naturally inspires us to expand.

Our environments physical, social, and emotional act like mirrors, reflecting our internal world back to us. If we live in clutter, chaos, or constant stress, our minds will echo that same disarray. But when we create peaceful spaces and set boundaries that protect our energy, we begin to feel more aligned and grounded.

For most of my life, I didn't realize how much the environments I chose were keeping me stuck. Whether it was a toxic relationship, an unfulfilling job, or even the energy of my living space, each reflected my internal beliefs about what I deserved. When I started shifting those beliefs choosing peace over chaos, calm over control everything began to change.

This is why self-awareness is so powerful. Once we understand that our beliefs, rules, and environments are shaping our reality, we can start consciously choosing new ones.

It's not easy. Rewriting your internal rulebook takes time, patience, and a lot of unlearning. But every small change every time you choose to believe something new about yourself or your world creates a ripple effect.

You begin to notice new opportunities. You attract people who align with your growth.

You stop settling for less than you deserve.

And most importantly, you begin to *trust yourself again.*

When I look back on my journey from the girl who felt trapped by depression and fear, to the woman who's learned to live, love, and trust freely, I see how every belief I once held served a purpose. Even the painful ones. They were stepping stones t at helped me discover who I truly am beneath all t e conditioning.

Our beliefs and rules are not permanent. They are simply programs we can rewrite when they no longer align with our truth.

The most freeing realization I've had is this: You don't have to keep believing what you were taught. You get to choose what to believe now.

You get to decide what success, love, and happiness mean for *you*. And once you do, your reality begins to shift in ways you never imagined possible.

Rewriting your Beliefs and Rules

Let's talk about the *how*.

In my case, I needed to change my environment because I wanted to get away from living for the weekends. I had had enough of feeling hungover, stuck and having negative feelings about myself.

Why did you pick up this book? What is not working in your life? And what are the rules that you've blindly followed that got you into your unique mess or circumstances?

You've probably realized by now that so many of the beliefs and "rules" you've been living by weren't created by *you*—not really. They were inherited, absorbed, or picked up through life experiences, childhood dynamics, cultural expectations, and even trauma. And for a while, they may have protected you. But just because something kept you safe once doesn't mean it's meant to stay with you forever.

Some rules you're living by right now may sound like:

- I have to work myself into the ground to be successful.

- If I don't make everyone happy, I'll be abandoned.

- I'm not smart enough to do what I really want.

- I can't trust people—they always let me down.

- If I let my guard down, I'll get hurt.

These rules operate in the background, subtly shaping your choices and keeping you stuck in patterns you don't even realize you're repeating.

So… how do we change them?

Step 1: Identify the Rule or Belief

The first step in rewriting each rule is becoming aware of it. This part can be uncomfortable because it requires honesty. Brutal honesty.

Start by paying attention to what triggers you or where you feel stuck. Ask yourself:

- What do I believe about this situation?
- What am I afraid might happen if I don't follow this rule?
- Where did this belief come from?

You might uncover something like, *I can't rest unless I've earned it.*

Where did that come from? A hardworking parent? A teacher who called you lazy? A culture that glorifies burnout?

Once you see the rule clearly, you've already begun to take back your power.

Step 2: Question Its Validity

Next, challenge the rules. Seriously question it like detective poking holes in a bad alibi.

Ask yourself:

- Is this belief actually true?
- Has this *always* been true?
- Who benefits when I believe this?
- What is this rule costing me?

For example, if your rule is "I have to be perfect to be loved", think about how many relationships have suffered under the weight of that pressure. Think about the love and connection you've missed out on by trying to perform instead of just being.

Step 3: Decide What You Want to Believe Instead

This is where it gets powerful. Now that you've spotted the rule and challenged it, it's time to *replace* it with something that aligns with who you are becoming.

But here's the key: your new belief needs to feel believable to your subconscious. You can't just go from "I'm worthless" to "I'm a goddess made of gold and moonlight" (though that would be nice). You need to build a bridge.

Instead of leaping too far, try creating "ladder beliefs" that move you step by step towards your desired reality.

For example:

- Old belief: I'm not good enough.
- Ladder belief: I'm learning to believe I'm enough.
- Final belief: I am more than enough exactly as I am.

Let your subconscious catch up. Speak the new belief out loud. Write it down. Put it on sticky notes. Repeat it every day until it becomes the rule you naturally live by.

Step 4: Reinforce Through Aligned Action

This is where your new rule becomes real, because belief without action stays a fantasy.

If your new belief is, "I deserve to be treated with respect," then you'll need to start speaking up, setting boundaries, walking away from disrespect, and surrounding yourself with people who reflect that new truth back to you.

Each time you act from this new belief, you reinforce it. You build evidence. And the old rule? It starts to lose its grip.

Step 5: Expect Resistance

Here's the thing: your old rules won't go down without a fight. They've been part of your inner operating system for years, maybe decades. So, when you start choosing differently, your brain might panic. Your body might feel anxious. People around you may push back.

That's okay.

Expect it. Normalize it. Let it be a sign that you're growing. The discomfort isn't a sign that you're doing it wrong—it's a sign that you're doing something *new*.

Step 6: Practice Self-Compassion

You're going to mess up. You're going to fall back into old patterns sometimes. That doesn't mean you've failed. It means you're human.

Be gentle with yourself.

This is deep, beautiful, transformational work. Every time you notice an old rule creeping back in, treat it like a signal—not a setback. Say to yourself, "Oh, I see you. But we're not doing that anymore."

That's how change happens. Not through perfection—through awareness, choice, and compassion.

Rewriting your rules isn't about pretending the past didn't happen. It's about choosing to no longer be ruled by it.

You get to decide what kind of life you want to live. You get to choose beliefs that empower you instead of limit you. And the most powerful truth of all?
You've had the pen in your hand this entire time.

So, here's what I want you to do: Start writing. Start rewriting. Start *living* by the rules *you* choose.

You are the author of your story. Make it one you're proud to live in.

Example Rule:

Let's take all of these steps, and I will break down a rule that I had about finishing this book.

Step 1: I've spent a lot of time procrastinating on finishing this book. I had to ask myself *why*, and I realized I had imposter syndrome. I didn't believe I was capable of writing anything and kept catching myself thinking, *Who would want to read this anyway?* My belief was that I didn't know enough and wasn't smart enough. My rule became that I needed to know more before I could finish this book.

Step 2: I had to ask myself if that was actually true. I reminded myself that I am smart and thought, Look at all the things you've already accomplished. I also realized that while I might not be where I want to be yet, this book could still help others who are just a chapter behind me.

I also used real-life examples of people who have written books before. I looked back at some authors' first books compared to their most recent books and saw how much they have grown and changed throughout the years.

Step 3: So, what was the new rule I put in place in order to help me finish this book. You have enough information that will help someone else.

Step 4: Every time I felt the procrastination start to kick in, I had to overcome it. Even if it meant just pulling out the manuscript and only writing one sentence. Just that small amount of action was helping me rewire that belief.

Step 5: I had so much resistance. I was fighting myself a lot and dragging my feet. I was so scared to put this book out there.

Step 6: I had to be kind to myself through this whole process. There were days when I would get extremely mad and beat myself up for not finishing it. Near the end of the editing process, I was working over forty hours a week. The job was physically demanding, and I was out in the heat all day. I'd get so upset when I couldn't think or write, even on my days off, and I'd end up sleeping instead. I had to practice compassion and remember that sometimes you truly need rest in order to think clearly. I also made the decision to go part-time so I could focus on this book and my own business. All of those steps worked—because you're now reading my final copy.

Every time you question an old rule, you take your power back. And trust me—you're stronger than any story you've ever outgrown.

Love

Learning Self-Love, Unconditional Love, and Love within Relationships

When I used to think about love, I believed it was all about falling in love with that special someone—the Hallmark movie kind of love, the picture-perfect, happily-ever-after romance you see in those sentimental films. I thought it was about finding a soulmate and living happily ever after. What I didn't realize is that love is much more complex and all-encompassing, with countless facets. It isn't just about romantic love; it's about how we show love to others, even to strangers, and, most importantly, to ourselves. In this chapter, I will explore the importance of self-love, unconditional love, and love in relationships.

Love Has Always Lived In Me

Unconditional love became a new concept for me over the past few years. It's a beautiful and complex idea—one that challenges us to love without judgment, without expectations, and without conditions. In a perfect world, we would show this kind of love to all beings. But as humans, our emotions and egos sometimes get in the way.

Looking back, I realise I've always had a strong capacity for unconditional love—just not for myself. As a child, I felt it for the natural world. I remember crying in school when I learned about deforestation, overwhelmed by the loss of trees I had never even seen. I felt it for strangers, sensing a deep, unspoken connection, though I rarely spoke of it, fearing I would be misunderstood.

The first time I consciously recognized this love in a relationship was with a partner, early in our time together. We hadn't yet said "I love you," but I felt a deep desire to support his dreams—even if it meant pausing my own for a while. His happiness mattered to me simply because it was his.

But unconditional love doesn't mean accepting harmful behaviour or staying in toxic situations. It means loving without judgment while knowing when to set healthy boundaries. This realization is what finally allowed me to turn that same love inward—to honour my needs, to protect my wellbeing, and to value myself as deeply as I valued others.

A great example of unconditional love is the love we feel for our pets—we do everything for them without expecting anything in return. It's the kind of love that doesn't fade based on actions or behaviour—it simply is. Learning to give that same steady, unshakable love to myself has been one of the most transformative shifts of my life.

Learning (and Unlearning) Love in Relationships

I've always dreamed of the sappy romantic love story—where you lock eyes from across a crowded room and feel an undeniable cosmic connection without saying a word. Where passion, heat, and romance never fade, and you stay in the honeymoon phase for life, living out the ultimate fairytale romance. But, like many things, I was told that this isn't realistic. Love and relationships take hard work and commitment.

Despite being a hopeless romantic, I found it difficult to find true love. I entered every relationship with the expectation that the other person would make me happy and solve all my problems. Unsurprisingly, this approach rarely worked out. My desperation for a fairytale ending caused me to overlook red flags, which would later contribute to the relationship's breakdown. My insecurities also played a big role, often sabotaging the connection. I used to think that love was a one-way street, with only my second half playing a role in making it work.

My people-pleasing tendencies, low self-esteem, and inclination to see the good in everyone made me fall for people too quickly. I would give everything for that person, often losing myself in the process. I had expectations of how love *should* look, but because I never communicated those expectations, I was left disappointed when the reality didn't match my fantasy. In the end, I realized that my happiness was my own responsibility—and that a relationship should *add* to my happiness, not be the sole source of it.

I also had to learn that I wasn't here to "fix" anyone. I believed that by loving someone deeply, I could help take away their pain and suffering. However, I now understand there are several flaws in that mindset:

- **Lack of acceptance:** I wasn't truly accepting my partner for who they were. I thought they needed to be more like me, with my "right" answers. This led to them feeling unworthy or "not enough." Imagine someone constantly telling you that you need to act a certain way—it doesn't feel good.

- **Ignoring red flags:** Because I wasn't seeing my partner for who they truly were, I overlooked behaviors that didn't align with my values. I thought I could change them to fit my ideal.

- **Judgment in disguise:** By trying to "fix" them, I was adding judgment to the relationship. This is not unconditional love.

- **Resentment:** Over time, this mindset caused resentment, ultimately leading to unhappiness for both parties involved.

The intention behind trying to change someone is rarely malicious, but it's not a healthy or sustainable mindset. We all have our own unique stories, and you can only control your own. It's important to remember that your beliefs about love shape your relationships.

When I learned to love and forgive who I was, the belief that I wasn't worthy of love dissolved. This also helped me release the story that people would try to change me. I finally understood that it's okay if some people don't like me or want to be with me. I knew my worth and trusted that the right person would come along.

These lessons didn't come overnight. It took a few painful reminders for me to really embody what self-worth looked like in love. One of those moments came with someone from my past.

I remember a guy I had been on and off with since high school. I finally ended things when I was twenty-eight. We met again after my divorce, and I quickly created a story in my mind: *Maybe this time, we could be together for good.* But after a few months of texting, I intuitively knew that something wasn't right. Turns out, he was just saying what I wanted to hear while secretly dating someone else. He made excuses for not seeing me, and when I called him out on it, he told me, "You can't visit because the town is too small, and it would ruin my reputation." He also said, "Good luck finding someone who'll put up with your lifestyle and travel the world with you."

Instead of reacting emotionally, I stood up for myself, wished him well, and never spoke to him again. It didn't hurt as much as it would have in the past because I finally respected and loved myself enough to know I deserved a better match. I remember telling him, "I will never be with someone again if it means losing who I am and not living by my values. I love myself too much to allow anyone to take away my power." That moment showed me that I would never allow myself to fall into an abusive relationship again. My subconscious had previously attracted such relationships because I didn't think I deserved love. Once I realized my worth, everything changed.

That experience became a turning point. It showed me what it felt like to choose myself, even when it hurt—and from that moment on, I started seeing love in a whole new way.

Have you ever heard the saying, "You find love when you're not looking for it?" It's so true. When we desperately search for the "perfect" person, we tend to overlook red flags. We settle for someone who doesn't meet our needs, or we fall in love with an idea of who they are rather than who they truly are. I spent years making excuses for the person I thought I loved, and in doing so, I caused myself more harm than good.

Eventually, I decided to get specific about what I wanted in a partner. I made lists and adjusted them as I dated different people. I learned how important the wording was in these lists. For example, I once listed "I want someone who wants to travel with me." When I asked an old partner about traveling, his response was, "What if I never get the chance?" It was a wake-up call to be more precise in my expectations. After that relationship, I refined my list to twenty-seven specific traits and, sure enough, I met someone who matched everything I had written down.

I realized that relationships don't have to be hard. When you're with someone who respects you and values your opinion, difficult conversations become easier. Yes, you'll still face challenges, but supporting each other makes it feel more manageable. The work I've done on myself has led to a healthier, "easier" relationship.

I used to believe that all relationships were chaotic, and if my partner didn't yell back at me, it meant they didn't love me. But now, I understand that a healthy relationship brings peace. You should feel calm around your partner, not always nervous.

Now that I had shifted the belief that relationships are hard, there was another belief around love that needed to be rewritten.

Once I'd made peace with my past and stopped chasing love, I realised there was still another story to rewrite—the one that told me lasting love didn't exist.

Love Always Fades

To shift my belief that "love always fades," I looked to other examples of lasting love. My nanna passed away twenty-one years ago, and my grandpa still loves her deeply after all that time. I also looked at the love my *second parents* have. They have been together now for forty-three years. The way they still look at each other with love and joy is admirable. I asked them what their secret was. They said it was open communication, mutual respect, forgiveness, and remembering to have fun. I had to ask myself, *why can't I have this too?*

One quality I added to my grandparents' list for a long, loving relationship is gratitude. Practicing daily gratitude for your partner is essential. It's easy to take each other for granted, especially with the distractions of daily life and social media comparisons. But when you pour into your relationship, both you and your partner will feel more fulfilled.

Have you ever had unrealistic expectations about what love needed to look like? I certainly have. I believed we needed to be intimate several times a day to prove we loved each other. Over time, I recognized that intimacy is not just physical. It's about vulnerable conversations and emotional connection.

Each person has a different way of showing love, so it's important to understand your partner's love language. By giving each other what you need to feel loved, you create a deeper, healthier bond. Remember, our brains are wired to prove our beliefs right. If you feel unloved, ask yourself whether your expectations are realistic or if you're unconsciously reinforcing old beliefs.

My New Rules for Love:

- I am worthy of love.
- The perfect partner for me exists.
- Relationships are fulfilling.
- The right person will love all of me and want to grow with me.
- Love is beautiful, and it's better to have loved than never to have loved at all.
- The honeymoon phase doesn't have to end.

The more I reflected on love through others—my grandparents, my mentors, my relationships—the more I saw that everything always came back to one thing: how deeply I loved myself. And that's where the real work began.

Coming Home to Self-Love

I still can't pinpoint the exact moment I fell out of love with myself. As children, we're born with a natural sense of self-love—but over time, life chips away at it. For me, it wasn't one big moment of loss; it was the slow accumulation of messages I absorbed from the world around me. Little comments, comparisons, and unspoken expectations shaped the way I saw myself. I started to believe that in order to be loved, I had to be *more*—blonder hair, thinner thighs, better grades, a quieter personality. Even my mom would casually say, "You'd be so much prettier if you dyed your hair lighter." She didn't mean any harm, but I took it to heart. And that's how it worked: one message after another, stacking up inside me like bricks. *You're not enough. You have to change. Be less. Be more.*

One of my earliest memories of this shift was in middle school, when I was fourteen. I had a huge crush on a boy, but couldn't even bring myself to talk to him. I had already convinced myself I wasn't good enough—not pretty enough, not smart enough, not popular enough. *Why would anyone want to be with you anyway?* The self-talk was brutal. I didn't have a single kind thing to say about myself. Looking back, I wish I could pinpoint the exact moment the self-love disappeared—but the truth is, it didn't vanish all at once. It eroded slowly, worn down by years of comparison, silence, and the stories I told myself about who I needed to be to be lovable.

It wasn't until I was twenty-nine, years into my healing journey, that I finally found self love again. I'll always remember the exact moment I realized, "Wow, I really do love myself."

The date was May 7th, 2022. I was hiking near Mount Shasta to a little lake called Heart Lake when I spotted a golf ball-sized rock. When I picked it up, I realized it was a pink quartz crystal. At the time, I didn't know much about crystals, but a friend I was with told me that pink quartz represents love. Tears started rolling down my face. I didn't care if my friend thought I was strange because I felt something I'd never felt before—unconditional love for myself. It almost felt like my heart wanted to explode.

That single moment cracked something open in me. From then on, self-love wasn't just a concept I talked about—it became the foundation for how I lived and how I related to everyone around me.

That experience showed me what my therapist had been telling me all along: *You cannot truly open your heart to love someone else until you learn to love yourself first.* Without self-love, relationships often become selfish. We end up depending on our partners to meet our needs and define our self-worth. We do things for them, but often with the expectation of getting something in return, instead of doing it purely to make them happy. And when that expectation isn't met, it breeds resentment.

Learning to love myself changed how I showed up in my relationships. I stopped dropping everything for friends who wouldn't do the same for me. I learned how to set boundaries with family and friends. And I soon realized that setting boundaries is one of the most powerful forms of self-love you can practice.

How I Rebuilt Self-Love (Step by Step)

Self-love didn't arrive all at once. It wasn't some grand awakening. It came through daily choices—small acts of devotion that added up over time.

I started showing up for myself the way I'd always shown up for others.

I took myself out on dates:
Picnics overlooking the Pacific. Solo movie nights. Dressing up just because. Even dancing, something that felt widely out of my comfort zone, became a ritual. Each moment told my subconscious: *You matter.*

I changed the way I dressed:

I let go of old clothes that held memories of who I used to be-the "fun party girl," the version of me who wore outfits to gain approval. I replaced them with pieces that made me feel powerful. At the time leather became my armor. Confidence became my aesthetic. Now it's sundress, embracing my more feminine side.

I practiced self-trust:

I realized I kept promises to others but constantly broke promises to myself. So I started small-one commitment a day. Wash the dishes. Take a walk. Send the email. Every completed task became a building block of trust.

I learned to set boundaries:

I stopped saying "yes" when I meant "no." I gave myself permission to protect my peace-even if it disappointed someone else. I wrote out my core values and used them as a compass. If something went against them, I didn't participate.

I forgave myself:

This was the hardest part. I carried a lot of guilt for things that happened in my past, things that made me feel unworthy of love. I blamed myself for the death of someone close to me. I blamed myself for the multiple sexual assaults I endured, thinking I was somehow at fault. I carried that shame for years, even blaming myself for not speaking up when I found out the same person had assaulted someone else. But healing meant letting go. Wrapping my younger self in love. Telling her, *You did the best you could. It was never your fault.* Forgiveness cracked the door open. Self-love walked through it.

That deep forgiveness became the final piece. It cleared the space for something new—a kind of love that flowed freely, without needing validation or approval.

Love is no longer something I chase-it's something I create, nurture and share. The deeper I fall in love with myself, the more I attract people who reflect that same love back. I no longer settle. I no longer shrink. I no longer mistake chaos for passion. Because now, I know: Love isn't loud or dramatic. Healthy love feels like peace.

Exercises:

1. Look at yourself in the mirror every morning and say, "I love you. I love everything about you—the good, the bad, and everything in between. I love who you are becoming." If it feels right, you can also include, "I forgive you."

2. Write out a list of everything you want in a partnership. Be very specific—what are their values, character traits, how do they treat you, how do you want your day-to-day relationship to look?

3. Reflect on your beliefs about love and relationships. Which beliefs might be holding you back from finding love? Are there unrealistic expectations or needs standing

in the way? Can you meet some of these needs yourself?

And as my understanding of love shifted, so did the way I related to the people in my life, setting the stage for everything I would soon learn about connection, boundaries, and rebuilding trust.

Relationships

Rewriting the Rules of Connection

Navigating relationships—whether they're romantic, platonic, familial, or professional—is rarely simple. For a long time, I believed there was a "right" way these connections should look. I created unspoken rules, shaped by past wounds and societal expectations, and clung to them without realizing how limiting they were.

The truth is that some relationships are meant to last forever—and others come into our lives simply to teach us something before they move on. Not everyone is meant to walk our entire path with us. Letting go—especially when we still love or care for someone—can feel like a quiet kind of grief, like watching a familiar sunset for the last time, knowing the light won't fall the same way again. But sometimes, growing means making room for peace, even if it means gently releasing the hands we once thought we'd hold forever.

Relationships With Friends and Colleagues

There was a time when I was consumed by what other people thought of me. I didn't want to rock the boat, so I kept quiet when something didn't feel right. I let people cross my boundaries—though at the time, I didn't even know what a boundary was. I was the "yes" person. The one who would drop everything to be there for others, even when I was running on empty.

I now realize that the reason I stayed in toxic friendships and one-sided connections for so long is that I hadn't yet learned the value of self-respect. I didn't know I was allowed to put myself first. Let me be clear: loving someone doesn't mean you have to tolerate being drained, used, or disrespected.

There was a turning point for me when a close friend pulled me aside and, with a mix of love and honesty, called out another friend I had been defending. He told me she was manipulating me, guilt-tripping me, and treating me like her personal punching bag. At first, I made excuses for her—telling myself (and him that she was just going through a tough time.

The truth was, I didn't want to take accountability for the fact that I was allowing someone to treat me that way. And honestly, I was scared of hurting her feelings. But eventually, I had to face the hard truth: no matter what someone is going through, it doesn't give her the right to constantly hurt or drain someone else. Period.

One of the hardest lessons I've had to learn was that we teach people how to treat us.

If you shrug off harmful comments, stay quiet when your boundaries are crossed, or keep picking up the pieces while never asking for support, then that becomes the standard. That's the dynamic you allow.

It took me time—and a lot of unlearning—but I started setting boundaries. Real ones. Some people didn't like it. Some relationships faded out. Others became stronger and healthier because of it.

And here's the thing: *choosing yourself doesn't mean you love them less. It means you love yourself more.*

Some friendships ended simply because we were no longer aligned. They stayed in environments I had outgrown. They wanted to stay comfortable, and I needed to keep evolving. That doesn't mean I don't wish them well. I still send them love from afar. But I had to let go of trying to belong in places where I no longer felt safe or supported.

This wasn't easy for me in the beginning. I wasn't expecting the sudden wave of grief that hit me. At first, I thought something was wrong with me because I kept finding myself in these cycles of crippling sadness—something that felt a lot like my depression. I mean, I was trying to grow and step into a new version of myself, so why did I feel like this?

It took me a while to let myself really feel it and realize that I was allowed to grieve. I was stepping away from people and environments that had once been a part of me, and it's okay to feel sad about that.

Family Boundaries

Family boundaries can be even harder, but just as necessary. Sometimes, the hardest people to set boundaries with are the ones closest to us. But doing so helped me create *healthier* relationships with family members—not colder ones. Sometimes, distance is what creates clarity.

My relationship with my dad is a perfect example of how creating distance can bring clarity. It wasn't an easy decision, but I was in the process of reframing my beliefs and building the life I had always dreamed of. My dad didn't agree with everything I wanted, and because I had such a deep-rooted desire to make him proud, that disagreement made things even harder.

For a while, going against his beliefs felt like I was betraying him, and that blocked me from fully stepping into my own. So, I created some space. That distance gave me the clarity I needed. I was finally able to stand in my truth—not from a place of reaction, but from a place of love.

When we reconnected, our conversations shifted. I wasn't as reactive or defensive anymore. I could actually hear what he was saying, and I could communicate where I was coming from in a way that helped him understand—not just what I was doing, but why. That space allowed both of us to grow and made our relationship stronger.

When I quit drinking, I lost a lot of friends. And while that was painful, it also showed me how many of those friendships were built around shared habits—not shared values. I walked away from people I cared about deeply because I no longer felt comfortable being in environments where heavy drug use was normalized. I wanted something different for my life, and that meant choosing discomfort over destruction.

Romantic Relationships

This section held me back from writing this book for a while. I kept thinking, *who am I to talk about healthy relationships when I've struggled to sustain one myself?* But the truth is, that's *exactly* why I can speak to it. I've lived through the chaos. I've stayed in toxic cycles. And now, for the first time, I'm in a relationship that feels safe—and I'm learning what love is supposed to look like.

My current partner and I have been together for over a year now and I'll be honest: sometimes it still feels foreign. I catch myself wondering, *when is the other shoe going to drop? When does the kindness stop? The support? The love? When do I lose myself again?*

Those thoughts come from old wounds and old programming. But now, each time one of these thoughts comes up, I use the STOP Thought Method—a cognitive-behavioral technique used to interrupt and eliminate unwanted, intrusive, or negative thoughts.

- "S" stands for Stop.
- "T" stands for Take a breath.
- "O" stands for Observe.
- "P" stands for Proceed.

This method helps bring awareness to the negative thoughts and reframes them into a more positive form. So, I turn the negative questions around and ask myself: *How good can it get? What if I let myself receive this kind of love?*

This man has taught me so much and has already helped heal many of my past wounds and trauma. I want nothing more than to spend the rest of my life with him, but if, for some reason, we are not able, I will always be thankful for him showing me what a true, healthy relationship looks like.

I used to think that love had to be chaotic. That if someone didn't fight back or yell with me, they didn't care. I confused passion with dysfunction because that's what I grew up seeing. And in previous relationships, I often picked fights just to feel something. When things were calm, I mistook it for boredom instead of peace.

But here's what I now know: *Healthy love feels like peace*—like sitting under your favorite tree listening to the creek go by, while breathing in the forest air. It feels safe. It feels steady. It doesn't make you question your worth or feel like you're walking on eggshells or dimming your light to avoid casting shadows.

In one past relationship, I was constantly told I was "too much"—too emotional, too affectionate, too needy. I remember reaching out for a hug and being shoved away with the words, "Don't touch me, bitch." Those words took root, and for a long time, I believed them.

But now? I've rewritten that rule: *The right person will never make you feel like you're too much.* They'll love all of you—your depth, your softness, your strength, your sparkle. They won't try to dim your light. They'll want to bask in it.

And maybe the biggest shift has been realizing that I don't lose myself in love anymore. Because I've done the work to *know* myself. And I've learned to hold onto my truth, even while building something beautiful with someone else.

My old rules around relationships:

- Relationships are chaotic, not safe. What I felt was more like survival than love.

- Speaking up for myself felt like a risk I couldn't afford. If I stand up for myself, I'll be abandoned.

- I taught myself I needed to shrink; I can't be my full self.

- To be chosen I made myself smaller and smaller. I always lose myself in relationships.

My new rules around relationships:

- Relationships can be safe, calm, and supportive, just like coming into a steady harbour.

- My truth is no longer something I hide-it's a light that draws in the right ones. My authenticity attracts aligned and meaningful connections.

- I no longer water myself down. I can be fully myself and be deeply loved for it.

- I am no longer searching to be completed, I stay rooted in who I am—love adds to me, not erases me.

Relationships will always require work, but not suffering. There's a difference. As you evolve, your connections will too. Some people will rise with you. Some won't. That's not failure—it's growth.

As you rewrite your beliefs about love, friendship, and connection, remember this: You deserve relationships that honor you, challenge you to grow, and allow you to feel safe. You don't need to earn love by shrinking yourself. You're worthy of connection just as you are.

The more you live from that truth, the more aligned your relationships will become.

Exercises:

1. Journal or meditate on these questions:

    - Have you been tolerating disrespect, manipulation, or emotional neglect from someone because it's easier than losing them?

- What are you afraid will happen if you set a boundary?

- Are your current beliefs helping you attract the relationships you want or keeping you stuck in what feels familiar but unhealthy?

- What beliefs were you taught about relationships growing up (from family, media, or culture)?

- Do any of those beliefs still show up in your adult relationships? If so, how? Now rewrite your new ones.

- What does a healthy boundary look like for you right now?

2. Now that you have determined what healthy boundaries look like, practice setting these boundaries in real life.

In the end, every lesson about love brought me back to the same truth: the relationship I build with myself shapes every connection that follows.

Money

Rewriting the Rules to Let Abundance Flow In

Let's talk about money. Not from a "how to budget" angle—but from the deep, emotional, sometimes shame-filled place we don't like to go. The part no one teaches us about: what money *represents*. Safety. Power. Guilt. Freedom. Self-worth. For most of my life, I had no idea just how tangled up my beliefs were when it came to money. I thought I was just being careful. Responsible. Modest. But the truth? I was afraid.

Afraid that money would change me. Afraid I wasn't worthy of having it. Afraid of what it meant if I did have money.

These thoughts and fears were blocking me from attracting the kind of wealth I truly wanted in my life. Maybe you're someone who's tired of living paycheck to paycheck. Maybe you're trying to change careers, start your own business, or you're simply exhausted from feeling anxious every time money comes up. If any of that sounds familiar, this chapter is for you.

During the writing process of this book, I had a couple of life-changing opportunities. One was joining a mastermind group to work with a renowned spiritual activator/coach, and the other was attending an entrepreneur trip with like-minded individuals. Both opportunities showed up around the same time, and both were incredibly terrifying for me. Partly because I knew I would be stepping far out of my comfort zone, but also because of the cost. These experiences required an investment I had never made in myself before—and at the time, I didn't have the funds available to cover it. So, I had no choice but to charge it to my credit card, which is something I had always avoided.

Until then, I had never carried a balance on a credit card, and I certainly had never invested that amount of money in my personal growth. To put it simply: I was scared. The total cost for both experiences came to about $15,000, and I had just two months to figure out how to pay it back. I had never earned more than $4,000 in a month before (and that was while I was in the military, living in California), so making that leap was terrifying. When you're trying to build a life in "untraditional" ways, that kind of financial pressure feels almost impossible.

But here's the truth—putting myself in that difficult situation was the best thing that could have happened. I was forced to find a way to pay off this debt quickly. It pushed me to reevaluate everything I had ever believed about money. This situation demanded a rapid shift in my mindset, and even though I had been working on my beliefs around money for over a year, this was the moment I was pushed to confront my fears head-on.

I had to confront the deep-rooted beliefs I had about money, which were ingrained in me over years of upbringing. These beliefs sounded like:

- Money is bad.
- I must work really hard to make money.
- People with a lot of money are not good people.
- I don't deserve to have a lot of money.
- Money changes people.

Many of these beliefs stemmed from my father. "You work hard for your money" was one of his favorite sayings. He came from a generation where you worked for the same company for decades, earned benefits like health insurance and a pension, and were promised a stable future if you put in the time. But today, that model no longer holds. The idea that working hard at a single job for a lifetime guarantees financial security is outdated, and deep down, I knew that was not the path I wanted to follow. Yet, despite my conscious awareness, my subconscious was still holding me back.

Changing our beliefs around money is essential if we want to attract it into our life, because our beliefs shape our reality. Whether we realize it or not, the way we think and feel about money influences how we earn it, ask for it, manage it, and even whether we allow ourselves to receive it at all.

If deep down we believe money is bad, or that having it makes us greedy, or that we don't deserve it, we'll subconsciously push it away. We might undercharge, overgive, avoid financial conversations, or miss opportunities because part of us doesn't feel safe having money. It's not because we're lazy or incapable—it's because our internal wiring is working against our external desires.

We can hustle as hard as we want, but if our subconscious beliefs are rooted in fear, scarcity, or guilt, we'll either repel money or find ways to lose it just as quickly as it comes. True, lasting wealth starts with alignment. When your beliefs support your goals, you can create the internal safety and self-trust needed to attract, hold, and grow your wealth in a way that feels good.

For years, I had tried to create passive income streams. I created online courses, shot videos, and even worked with clients, but I could never bring myself to ask for what I was worth. I'd work with people for free or charge pennies for my time. I'd do odd jobs here and there, but never ask for money, simply appreciating whatever was given to me in return. I even gave away more products than I sold, all because I was terrified of money.

The fear wasn't just about the money itself—it was about what it represented. I feared that to make a lot of money, I would have to sacrifice my time, my energy, and my values. I feared that if I became financially successful, I would lose sight of what mattered most to me—helping others and protecting the environment. I didn't trust myself to manage wealth without being corrupted by it. I thought that having money would change me, make me "bad," or drive me to work endlessly in the pursuit of more.

I realized that I was trapped in this cycle of self-sabotage, perpetuated by limiting beliefs. If I didn't address these fears and shift my mindset, I would continue to struggle with money for the rest of my life. This was the pivotal moment that forced me to examine my beliefs and take action.

As I began to face my fears about money, I realised I'd been living by inherited rules—ones that said security had to come through struggle and that wealth came with guilt. It was time to rewrite those rules.

So, how did I overcome it? I had to prove my subconscious wrong by seeking out examples of people who were making money *and* using it for good. One of the most powerful moments came from the entrepreneur trip. I met so many incredible people who were making money by doing purpose-driven work. These individuals showed up as their authentic selves, and money hadn't changed them—it had empowered them to help others. They were living proof that money could be a force for good, and they made me realize that I could do the same. I just had to trust myself again and stop fearing what money might do to me.

I also realized that to continue helping others and protecting the planet's natural resources, I *needed* money. We are all living a human experience, and within that experience, we need money to survive and to thrive. If I'm constantly stressing about money, how could I possibly show up for others in the way I wanted to? By choosing to embrace wealth, I could not only provide for myself but also create the means to help more people and make a bigger impact.

Additionally, I sought out examples of people who weren't working themselves into the ground to make money. I saw that it was possible to build systems and create passive income streams that would allow me to work smarter, not harder. Yes, there are times when hard work is necessary, but ultimately, I wanted to create a life where I could generate money while maintaining my autonomy. I wanted to be able to build something for myself, rather than working for someone else.

Through all of this, I had to rebuild my trust in myself. I had to believe that I deserved wealth, that I could handle it responsibly, and that it wouldn't change me in the ways I feared. In the chapter about worthiness, I go into more detail about how I did this. But for now, here are the new beliefs I adopted about money:

- Money can help me help more people and protect the environment.

- Money flows to me easily and effortlessly.

- There are many good people on this planet who make a lot of money and use it for good.

- I have exactly what I need.

I came to understand that to receive more money, I had to address the subconscious blocks I had around it. Without changing these underlying beliefs, I could make money, but I would likely lose it just as quickly, falling back into the same patterns of scarcity. This is why so many lottery winners end up bankrupt within a few years. Despite winning millions, they never resolve their subconscious issues around money, and often find themselves in a worse financial situation than they were before.

Exercises:

- **Examine your money beliefs:** Write down the thoughts and beliefs you have about money that may be holding you back. Think of a few real-life examples that disprove these beliefs. Then, rewrite your new beliefs in a positive, empowering way. Read them every morning for a month to help reprogram your subconscious.

- **Appreciate what you have:** Instead of focusing on the lack of money, start appreciating all the money that is already coming into your life. Thank it every day. This simple practice shifts your focus from scarcity to abundance.

- **Affirmations:** Here are some of my favorite positive affirmations around money:

    - I am a money magnet.

    - Money flows easily and effortlessly towards me.

    - I am grateful for money and the opportunities it brings.

Wherever you're starting from, trust that your relationship with money can evolve in a healthy, grounded way. One gentle shift at a time, you're teaching your mind—and your life—that it really is safe to receive more.

Business and Success

Defining It for Ourselves

If you're reading this book and, in particular, this chapter, chances are you're at a crossroad or maybe you've already taken the leap. You're doing something bold. Unconventional. Something that might not make sense to everyone around you. So, ask yourself, "What choice or dream am I stepping into that others may not understand?"

Maybe you're building a business from the ground up. Maybe you've left a stable career to pursue something more meaningful. Or maybe you're just waking up to the idea that success doesn't have to look the way you were taught it should.

Wherever you are on your journey, I want you to know this: You're not alone.

At thirty, I found myself making a huge career change—one I never imagined I'd pursue, and honestly, one I didn't believe was possible for a long time. I wasn't following the well-worn path anymore. I was finally choosing to follow my purpose: helping others while building something of my own. That decision brought a deep sense of freedom; it also cracked open a world of fear.

Take a moment to imagine what following your purpose would look like in your life? What fears come up for you when you think about choosing your own path?

Because stepping outside the "safe" box of how things are *supposed* to be done shakes things up, people start projecting their own doubts, fears, and limitations onto you. Sometimes it's subtle. Sometimes it's loud and direct. But either way, it's tough—especially when those voices come from people you love.

Who in your life is projecting their fears onto you? Have their doubts influenced the decisions you've made? It's important to remember not to place blame when you ask yourself these questions. Most people aren't coming from a place of malintent; they're simply projecting their own fears onto you. But gaining awareness of where your beliefs and thoughts come from is what allows you to rewrite them.

So let's redefine success—not by society's standards, but by your own.

What follows is a look at my journey of doing just that. It hasn't been easy. It's taken deep trust, patience, and a lot of unlearning. But the freedom, alignment, and fulfillment I've found by staying true to myself? That's a version of success I wouldn't trade for anything.

One of the biggest emotional hurdles in this process has been learning how to stay true to myself while still wanting to make my dad proud.

He simply doesn't understand why I'm choosing this path. We've had countless conversations, and he still asks when I'm going to get a "real" job. He worries I'm making a huge mistake. He tells me, "You know, you're going to have to work even harder owning your own business than if you worked for someone else."

And I get it. I really do.

When I was younger, my dad started his own construction company. He built beautiful homes, poured himself into the work, and faced challenge after challenge. But when the 2008 financial crisis hit, he lost everything. He filed for bankruptcy and had to rebuild his life from scratch. I've never seen anyone fight harder to support their family, and I will always admire that.

He taught me to work hard. To never give up. That no matter how far you fall, you can rise again. But here's what I've come to realize: His lessons don't have to define my path.

My dad's generation grew up believing the corporate job was the golden ticket—the safest, most responsible choice. He views entrepreneurship as risky and unstable, and thinks my generation lacks the work ethic to persevere.

He is convinced that no one wants to work these days. That they just want everything handed to them. But there's a flaw in that thinking.

The truth is, the world has changed. You used to be able to stay at one company for decades, earn a pension, and retire comfortably. But now? Pensions are vanishing, job security is a myth, and even people who've given twenty years to a company can get laid off in an instant.

I have friends with so-called "good jobs" who are still barely getting by. Some take on second jobs just to cover the basics. People are living to work—not working to live.

Every day, they rush out the door, battle traffic, put in their eight hours, fight more traffic on the way home, and by the time they walk through the front door, they're running on empty. There's just enough energy to microwave dinner, maybe squeeze in a quick workout, and fall into bed. And then it starts all over again.

For many, the weekend is the only time they get to exhale. Maybe a two-week vacation if they're lucky.

I made a conscious choice to leave the military after I'd realized that I didn't want that life. I couldn't do it. I wanted something more.

Breaking free from that rhythm—the one I now call the "matrix"—wasn't just a career change. It was a mental, emotional, and spiritual shift. But it didn't come easy. I battled myself every day with thoughts like:

- Maybe I should just work for someone else while I get this business going. That way, I'll have a steady income.

- What if I lose everything?

- Do I really want to work more hours for myself than I would for someone else? What happens to my freedom?

- Who's going to want to work with me? I can't make money doing this.

Those thoughts were constant. Loud. And honestly? Tempting. But deep down, I knew: If I took the easy route, I'd never follow through on my dreams. I'd never build the coaching business I was so deeply called to create. So I let go of the backup plan. Because having a backup plan felt like telling myself I wasn't going to succeed.

I made peace with the idea of losing it all. I told myself, *Even if I fail, I'll figure it out.*

My dad lost everything and rebuilt. So have countless others. Some of the most successful people I admire have lost everything—more than once—and still found their way back. Failure isn't the opposite of success. It's part of it.

It has taken me three years to get my business and my mindset to where I want them to be. The journey has been full of ups and downs, and there were moments when I panicked because I had no money coming in and still had bills to pay.

I hit a point where I lost all of my clients and had to rebuild—then rebuild again. If I had listened to my old beliefs and all the negative thoughts, I would've given up. Plenty of people told me to let it go, that it wasn't working, but I just couldn't do it.

I remind myself every day why I chose this path: To gain time freedom. To live life on my own terms. To create a life that actually feels like *mine*.

And that required changing how I view success—completely.

I used to believe success looked like this:

- Making over $100,000 a year

- Working a 9–5 job at a well-known company

- Earning a PhD

- Holding a high-ranking title

Here's the problem: While I was in the military, most of those goals felt out of reach. I wasn't climbing the same ladder as my peers in corporate America. I felt behind, and that sense of "not measuring up" took a toll on my self-esteem. I was constantly beating myself up for not doing enough. But then I realized: What if those goals weren't mine to begin with? What if I could define success for myself? That shift changed everything.

Here's what success looks like for me now:

- I know I'm successful when I can stay present and enjoy quality time with the people I love.

- I know I'm successful when I prioritize self-care and meet my own needs, so I can show up fully.

- I know I'm successful when I no longer feel guilty about taking time to rest and recharge.

- I know I'm successful when I have the freedom to do things that bring me joy and fulfillment.

- I know I'm successful when I leave people better than I found them—with a smile, a kind word, or a meaningful moment.

- I know I'm successful when I help others reach their goals without draining my own cup.

- I know I'm successful when I can give generously and live in abundance.

- I know I'm successful when I let go of needing external validation—and simply do what makes me happy.

These aren't far-off dreams. These are things I can choose every single day. Even on the hard days, I set an intention to brighten someone's day—because that, to me, has an impact. My morning routine is sacred. It helps me fill my own cup before pouring into others. Meditation grounds me, keeps me present, and quiets the noise in my head.

I'm no longer constantly consumed by doubt. I'm living in alignment, and that alignment has allowed me to feel confident in my decisions and see the results in my business that I'd been working toward. By shifting my mindset about what success looks like, I was able to detach from the pressure to achieve specific outcomes. When we release the negative feelings, stress, and desperation, we open ourselves up to actually receiving what we've been wanting all along.

Success is different for everyone. For some, it's a mansion and a private jet. For others, it's simply being able to pick their kids up from school or have dinner with their family each night.

It doesn't matter if you work in a corporate office, flip burgers, or run your own company. What matters is this: Can you master your emotions? Can you stay grateful and grounded in the small moments?

Because for me? That's where real success lives.

Exercises:

- **Find role models:** Look for people who are already doing what you want to accomplish. Use them as proof that it's possible. Ask yourself, "If they can do it, why can't I?"

- **Revisit your definition of success:** What are your current beliefs and rules about success? Which ones feel heavy or limiting? Rewrite those rules in a way that feels light and empowering. Make sure to include at least one thing you can accomplish every day that brings you closer to your version of success.

- **Overcome your business fears:** If you're starting your own business or purchasing a business, identify the rules and beliefs that are holding you back. Look for examples that prove those fears wrong. Rewrite them to support your journey toward success.

- **Envision your life:** Write down how you want your day-to-day life to look while operating or owning your own business. As you write, feel it as if it's already happening. Get detailed—what are your employees or teammates like, if you have any? How many customers do you need in order to make enough to live the life you want? What is your total yearly net income? Afterward, ask yourself:

What is the first action I can take today to make this happen?

Whatever your path looks like from here, let it be one that feels true to you. That's where real success begins and where it keeps growing.

Time

Rewriting Our Rules to Get Time Back

Time is one of the most powerful illusions we live by. We treat it like a fixed thing, something outside of us, always running out, something we have to chase. But the truth is, our experience of time is shaped by what we believe about it. When we believe there's never enough, we live in constant scarcity. But when we shift that belief to *I have more than enough time for what matters,* everything begins to open up. Our focus sharpens, our energy expands, and somehow, time starts to stretch.

This chapter is especially for the dreamers, creators, entrepreneurs, and visionaries who feel like they "never have enough time" to build the life or business they know they're meant for. It's for the ones juggling a job, a dream, a healing journey, and still telling themselves they're behind.

So, if you're someone who's craving more time in your day to do the things you love, pursue your passions, or finally start that business, this section is for you.

Our perception of time is a funny thing. When we're waiting for the two minutes it takes for our food to cook in the microwave, it drags on endlessly. Or that feeling of holding a plank for just sixty seconds, but still having another thirty seconds to go, which feels like an eternity. But when we're hanging out with friends or loved ones, a few hours can pass in the blink of an eye.

Even if you don't subscribe to the idea that "time doesn't actually exist, and that at any moment we can quantum leap into a different reality, because all realities co-exist," you can still examine your beliefs about time. By doing so, you can create new rules around how you experience it.

Because this is what this chapter is really about: the invisible rules you're living by when it comes to time, and how to consciously rewrite them.

I've come to believe that time is an illusion not just as a concept, but as something I've experienced deeply. There have been moments in my life where time seemed to stretch or collapse: a single hour that felt endless during struggle, or a whole day that passed in what felt like the blink of an eye when I was in flow. Those moments made me start questioning what time actually is. Is it real, or is it simply something our minds create to make sense of change?

When you start to look into it, science actually backs up this idea. Quantum physicists have found that on the most fundamental level, time doesn't behave the way we experience it. Einstein himself showed through his theory of relativity that time isn't constant; it bends and stretches depending on speed and gravity. Two people moving at different speeds or experiencing different gravitational pulls will actually experience time differently. That's not just philosophy; that's actual physics.

More recently, experiments in quantum mechanics like those exploring entanglement, suggest that all moments might coexist simultaneously. In quantum theory, particles don't have fixed positions or times until they're observed. That means "past" and "future" may not be as separate as we think. Physicist Carlo Rovelli thinks that time is not a fundamental feature of the universe at all, but something that emerges from our limited perspective as conscious beings.

When I read this and then looked at my own experiences, it clicked: the illusion of time isn't about denying that clocks tick, it's about realizing that our experience of time is flexible. We've all felt it. Meditation, creativity, love, grief—all of these can expand or compress our sense of time. Studies in neuroscience have shown that when we're in "flow," our brain's prefrontal cortex (the part responsible for self-monitoring) quiets down, and time perception fades. It's as if our attention to our own presence removes the need for time.

So when I say time is an illusion, I mean that we've mistaken a mental construct for an absolute truth. Time helps us organize our lives, yes—but it's not something outside of us; it's something we generate. And once you start to see it that way, you realize you can play with it, stretch it, slow it down, and even use it to your advantage.

This is where the old rules begin to fall apart.

Many of us wake up already rushing. We dash out the door and hit heavy traffic, making us late for work. We often feel like there's never enough time. The list of things we'd love to do is long, yet we rarely find the time to actually do them. We think, "There just isn't enough time in the day, let alone the week or the year, to get everything done." And so we sit, stuck in a cycle of inaction. By changing these thoughts, you start to take the actions that will provide the time you need.

When was the first time you remember feeling like you were "behind" or running out of time? Who or what taught you that?

My stepmom often jokes, "You Lee's get more time in a day than a normal human." She's not exaggerating. My dad seems almost superhuman when it comes to time management. I've never met anyone who can accomplish as much in a single day as he does. He's juggling physical labor, working on five different projects, and finishing them all in one day. Most people would take an entire day to finish just one of those tasks. My brother is the same way. When he tells me everything he accomplishes in a day, I just stare at him, wide-eyed, asking, "How? How is that even possible?"

Sure, it helps that they both wake up around 3:30 a.m. most days, but still, the amount they get done is nothing short of impressive. (Don't worry, I don't wake up nearly as early as they do—usually between 5:00 and 6:00 a.m.)

My friends often tell me that when they hang out with me, it feels like they've crammed three days into one. My old roommate in California used to ask, "Do you ever sleep?" The answer is "yes"—I aim for at least eight hours of sleep a night.

But there are a few reasons why it feels like I get more done than others. Over the years, I've worked on my time management, set clear intentions for the day, and shifted my mindset about how I view time. What I really did was this: I rewrote the rules I was living by.

Rule #1: "There is never enough time."

Before we dive into how to get your time back, it's important to look at the beliefs you hold about time itself. Your beliefs shape how you experience it. If you believe there's never enough time, you'll constantly feel rushed and behind. But if you believe time expands for what truly matters, you'll begin to notice moments stretching and opening up in ways that seem almost magical.

Beliefs are the foundation of every action we take. When we think time controls us, we move reactively, jumping from one task to the next, multitasking, and never feeling caught up. But when we shift the belief to, *I create time through my choices and focus*, we start to reclaim our power. Time stops being something that happens to us and becomes something we work with intentionally.

Getting your time back isn't just about better scheduling; it's about aligning your beliefs, habits, and energy. The following steps, blocking time, staying present, and setting intentions, are simple but powerful ways to bring that alignment into your daily life. When you combine practical tools with empowering beliefs, you begin to realize that you've always had enough time; it just needed to be reclaimed.

It's not time that overwhelms us; it's the rules we've attached to it.

Here are some old beliefs I had regarding time:

- I'm running out of time.
- Success has to happen fast or it doesn't count.
- Other people are ahead of me.
- I need to rush, or I'll fall behind.

These beliefs left me with anxiety every single day. I would spend hours stuck in my head, feeling the pressure I had put on myself, which only led me to take no action at all. That left me feeling even more behind, with added layers of shame and anger at myself for not doing enough. I was living in a constant state of negative emotions.

But once I shifted my beliefs around time, it felt like a weight lifted off my shoulders. I started noticing that I could actually get more done. Those little wins added up and turned me into the "superhuman" my stepmom always believed us Lees to be.

Here are my new beliefs around time:

- I'm always right on time for my journey.

- Sustainable success builds at the pace that's meant for me.

- I'm not in competition with anyone's timeline but my own.

- Rushing disconnects me from clarity. Presence moves me faster.

Which old rule about time do you feel ready to let go of today? Which rewritten belief feels the most freeing to you?

Rule #2:
"I don't have time to build the life I want."

Step One: Blocking Time

There was a time when I wasted so much time and had zero time management skills. To change that, I spent a week tracking every second of my day. I wrote it all down to see where I was wasting time, and more importantly, to create space for new habits I wanted to add to my routine. This exercise forced me to be honest with myself—there's no point in fudging your own timecard. It might seem tedious (and it is), but it brings much-needed awareness to how you actually spend your time.

I couldn't believe how much time I spent aimlessly scrolling through social media. I used to pride myself on not watching much TV, but I discovered that I was spending four to five hours a day on my phone. FOUR TO FIVE HOURS! Just looking at other people's lives and wishing I could do what they were doing. Clearly, I wasn't living in the present moment, nor was I appreciating how wonderful my own life was. So, I set timers for all my social media accounts, helping me be more intentional about how much time I spend on each platform. This alone freed up a couple of hours for more meaningful tasks.

This was the moment I realized: I didn't need "more time." I needed a new relationship with time.

I also started time-blocking my days. I'd dedicate specific blocks of time to certain tasks and never work on something for more than an hour without taking a 15-minute break. Those breaks allowed me to get up, move around, and reset my brain. Time-blocking also helped me stop multitasking, which I used to think was a good thing. However, I learned that multitasking actually drains energy because our brains must jump between tasks. This is why I keep my phone on "Do Not Disturb" while working—the constant notifications break my focus and make it take longer to get back on track. That 15-minute break is when I check my phone and respond to messages. These strategies have helped me get more done in less time.

Now ask yourself, are your current habits supporting the life you want? Or are they quietly stealing the time you need to build it?

If you reclaimed just ONE hour a day, what would you do with it to move your dream forward?

Would you finally start the business…
Learn a new skill…
Be more present with your kids…

What would the "future you" beg you to use that hour for?

Rule #3: "The future is more important than the present."

Step Two: Staying Present

Staying present throughout the day can also give you the illusion that your day is longer. It's true—we lose time by worrying about things that happened in the past or might happen in the future. Before I learned to take control of my thoughts, I spent hours lost in my head, not paying attention to anything around me. Ever wonder why time seems to stretch when you're on vacation in a new place? It's because you're fully present, engaged with what's happening around you, and enjoying each moment.

This is where your power lies: not in controlling the future, but in choosing how you show up right now. If you can shift your relationship with the present moment, you shift your entire relationship with time.

Every time you choose to stay aware of the present moment, you rewrite the belief that happiness and success live somewhere "later."

Where in your day can you practice being ten percent more present?

Rule #4:
"I don't have enough time to do this well."

Step Three: Setting Intentions

Setting intentions before a task can surprisingly give you more time too. Setting intentions is a powerful tool, not just for time management, but for all kinds of goals. For example, when I start a homework assignment, I'll set the intention that it will only take me two hours, and that I'll find all the resources I need right away. When I don't do this, it often takes me longer just to find the sources. If you constantly think you don't have enough time to finish something, then this belief is creating that reality of not having enough time.

This happens because our beliefs shape our outcomes. If you constantly think you don't have enough time to finish something, you're unintentionally reinforcing that scarcity in your actions. By consciously setting an intention, you're rewriting that belief: you're telling yourself that you do have enough time and resources to complete the task. Over time, these small belief shifts transform how you experience your day and what you feel capable of achieving.

Take one task you've been putting off this week. Before you start, write down your intention for how long it will take and how you will approach it. Notice if simply setting this intention changes your focus, energy, or confidence.

Setting intentions is not just about productivity; it's an act of self-trust. It's you telling yourself: I believe I am capable. I believe there is space for me. I believe I am not behind.

What is one task you will start today by setting an empowered intention first?

Rule #5:
"I should be further ahead by now."

There Is No Timeline for Success

Many of us fall into the trap of setting timelines for ourselves, thinking we need to achieve certain things by certain ages. I'm thirty-one, living out of my car, traveling the world with my dog, and starting several businesses. I've been told many times that I need to settle down, get a "real" job, and start a family because "you're not getting any younger." But I remind myself that we're all on different paths, and there's no one-size-fits-all timeline.

Watching my cousins and younger brother get married sometimes makes me feel like I'm "behind" in life, but then I realize there's no universal timeline for success. The right people and opportunities will come at the right time.

This is one of the most dangerous rules we live by: the idea that there is a "correct" timeline for life's most significant events.

It's okay to start over and try new things, no matter your age. Too often, we let societal timelines or other people's expectations hold us back from exploring new passions or reinventing ourselves. I used to believe that if I hadn't mastered something by a certain age, I'd never be good at it, or that trying something new later in life was pointless or even reckless.

But life has a way of teaching us differently when we're open to learning and growing. That's where rewriting beliefs comes in. We can question the rules we've been taught—like "I need to have it all figured out by twenty-five" or "trying something new later in life is too risky" and replace them with beliefs that serve us, like "I am always capable of growth and learning" and "It's never too late to start."

Here's one story that completely changed how I view timelines and possibilities:

When I was in elementary school, I had a friend who seemed incredibly cool. She played ice hockey, was good at any sport, and even snowboarded. We lived in North Carolina, so snowboarding felt like the ultimate skill. I remember wishing I could be just like her. During a Girl Scout ski trip, she and a few others went snowboarding. I wanted to join them, but my mom insisted I take a ski lesson instead. She told me

I wasn't coordinated enough for snowboarding and that I should just stick to the bunny hill. I was terrible at skiing, so I gave up on snowboarding for years, convinced I'd never be good at it.

But when I moved to California at twenty-seven, only three and a half hours away from Lake Tahoe, I decided to give snowboarding another shot. I asked a friend to join me for a group lesson. I fell in love with it that day. I bought my own gear and a season pass, and for the next three winters, I practically lived in the mountains. I'd go up most weekends, teaching myself to get down the mountain.

The point of this story is that it's never too late to try new things. By challenging the belief that I was "too old" or "not good enough," I rewrote the rules I'd been living by. I had people ask, "Aren't you a little old to be trying that?" They predicted I'd get hurt, but I didn't care. Each time I went up, I got a little better, and now I can make it down a black diamond without falling. I'm nowhere near great, but I'm improving every time I practice, and I won't give up.

What is one thing you secretly want to try again or for the first time, but have told yourself it's "too late" for?

In many places, we're forced to change our clocks twice a year. If someone else can change time for us, we can certainly influence how we experience it.

We can take control over how we manage and perceive time. Remember, time is an illusion, and we're all on our own unique journey. Don't get caught up comparing yourself to others or thinking you need to achieve certain milestones by a specific age.

By questioning old rules and rewriting limiting beliefs, you give yourself the freedom to try new things, grow at your own pace, and create your own timeline for success. You're not behind, you're exactly where you're meant to be. It's never too late to try something new. And from this place of self-trust, time no longer controls you. You begin to move in partnership with it.

When you trust your own timing, time stops feeling like something you are running out of and becomes something you are finally in sync with.

Exercises:

- **Track your time:** For a week, document the hours you're awake. See where you're spending time and categorize it (work, emails, chores, time with family/friends, etc.).

- **Mindset awareness:** Pay attention to how you view time. When you feel stressed or like there isn't enough time, take a few deep breaths and remind yourself: *I have enough time. It will all work out, and I am in control.*

- **Set intentions:** Before starting any task, set a clear intention for how long it will take and what you aim to accomplish. This simple practice can help you feel more focused and efficient.

- **Rewrite your new rules around time:** From

this moment on, I choose to believe that time _____.

Wherever you find yourself with time, let it be guided by presence and intention. That's where real freedom begins—and where the value you place on yourself starts to shine.

Reclaiming Your Worth

You Were Always Enough

This chapter is for the person who has spent years carrying the quiet, heavy belief that they are not enough. For the overthinker who second-guesses every decision. For the high achiever who does everything "right" yet still feels unworthy. For the people-pleaser who bends, stretches, and shrinks themselves just to feel accepted. For the one who can pour love into everyone else but struggles to offer even a drop to themselves.

It's for you if you've ever felt like you had to earn your worth through productivity, perfection, your body, your success, or someone else's approval. It's for you if you're exhausted from trying so hard. It's for you if you're ready to stop performing and start being.

Or if you are an entrepreneur, coach, creative, or purpose-driven leader, this belief may be costing you more than you realize. It's the reason you undercharge, overwork, doubt your message, avoid visibility, or play small when you are meant to lead.

This chapter is your invitation to finally put down the belief that you are not enough and remember the truth you were born with: You were always worthy. You just learned to forget the value of your contribution to every interaction you've participated in.

Why do we so often feel like we're not enough?

It's important to understand this: the way you feel about yourself today didn't come from nowhere. You learned it. Someone, intentionally or not, taught you the rules you're still living by. This chapter is where we examine those old rules, see where they came from, and begin writing new ones that reflect your truth, not your conditioning.

This is not just emotional healing. This is about rewriting the internal rules that shape how you lead, create, and take up space in the world.

Most of us spend our lives chasing enoughness outside of ourselves, trying to prove to others that we're worthy, hoping that if they believe it, maybe we finally will too.

Let's get real for a moment.
How many times have you thought:

- *I'm not good enough.*

- *I'm too much.*

- *If I were different—prettier, smarter, more successful—then maybe I'd be lovable.*

- *I have to earn my worth.*

If those thoughts feel familiar, you're not alone. I used to live in that mental space every single day. Quietly doubting myself, questioning whether I was lovable or worthy unless I proved something. Unless I achieved something. Unless I became someone better.

What I didn't realize for a long time was this: worth isn't something you earn. It's something you already are. I had to unlearn that societal belief that told me my value depended on what I achieved.

When we grow up in environments that attach worth to performance, appearance, obedience, or achievement, we learn to tie our value to external things. Over time, we start to believe that being ourselves isn't enough.

That belief doesn't just sit quietly in our mind—it shows up in every area of our life. For me some were:

- I stayed in toxic relationships because I

thought that's all I deserved.

- I don't ask for the raise because I am scared of being seen as greedy.

- I overextend myself just to prove my value.

- I shrink in rooms where I should be shining.

In my work, it showed up as undercharging, overdelivering, doubting my message, and holding back from fully owning the space I was meant to step into. I watched myself dim my light in moments where I should have been leading.

Where Does the "Not Enough" Story Begin?

The "not enough" story isn't really a story; it's a rule someone else wrote for you, long before you knew you had the power to write your own.

Most of us didn't wake up one day and decide we weren't enough.

This belief started somewhere, maybe in childhood, through a passing comment, an emotionally unavailable parent, a teacher who made you feel small, a moment when your feelings were dismissed.

It could look like when you mispronounced that word and were corrected and embarrassed in public, you were misunderstood or disagreed with, even if you were right at the time. This is how the small doubts add up and each small fear clusters together. To make you doubt your worth.

Even something as subtle as being praised only when you performed well can train your brain to associate your worth with doing, rather than simply being. This one still shows up in my own life. I often find it hard to rest or slow down because I've tied busyness and achievement to my sense of self-worth. That belief was formed early on, watching how hard my dad worked and hearing him praise effort and productivity above all else. I have to remind myself all the time that it's okay to rest and resting is not being lazy.

That is when I finally recognized the rule I was living by, "My worth depends on how hard I work." Once I was able to name it, I could challenge it. I could rewrite it into something true: "My worth exists even when I rest."

This is the exact process of rewriting the rules: identify the old rule, challenge it, and replace it with a new truth.

Those moments become unspoken rules we live by, rules like "my worth depends on how well I perform," or "I'm lovable only when I'm pleasing others." But the thing about rules is this: they are not truths. They're learned. And anything learned can be rewritten.

This is how rewriting the rules begins, by seeing the old ones clearly enough to choose something more appropriate and empowering.

The "not enough" belief is sneaky.

It can sound like:

- I'll feel better about myself once I lose weight.

- I'll be happy when I finally get that promotion.

- I'll finally feel confident once I'm in a relationship.

But let's be honest—even when those things happen, it's never enough for long. That's because worthiness doesn't come from anything out there. It comes from within.

I used to think that I had to look a certain way to be enough. Growing up, I was constantly told that I looked better with a tan and that my hair needed to be blonder. My looks were constantly being picked at. A few years ago, I didn't let myself tan or dye my hair because I wanted to fall in love with all of me, not an image I thought I had to uphold.

It can also sneak up on you in the form of self-sabotage. I had a client who, when things started going too well for them, would ruin it. They didn't believe that they deserved a good life. It showed up in the form of quitting jobs when they finally started to become financially stable, or even trying to ruin their relationship because they didn't think they truly deserved love like that.

And then one day, they chose differently. Even though the fear was still there, they stayed. They kept the job. They allowed the relationship to be good. They started acting as if they were worthy of stability—and slowly, their reality began to match that belief.

Don't worry, you too can rewrite this damaging belief.

Before we can rewrite a belief, we have to recognize it for what it truly is: a rule we internalized without conscious consent. These rules shape how we show up, how we love, how we chase success, and even how we treat ourselves. But they are just that, "Rules". Learned. Inherited. Absorbed. And rules can be challenged. They can be replaced. They can be rewritten into ones that reflect your worth instead of your wounds.

You are not broken. You are just living by outdated rules.

The 4-Step Process for Rewriting the "Not Enough" Rule

The first step in reclaiming your worth is acknowledging that somewhere along the line, you learned to disconnect from it. This is not about blaming others; it's about understanding where the story began, so you can finally stop carrying it.

Ask yourself:

- Where did I first learn that I wasn't enough?
- Whose voice does this belief sound like?
- What was happening in my life when I started feeling this way?

Bringing it into awareness doesn't fix it overnight, but it's the first step into cracking the walls of your self imposed prison.

The next step is to grieve the false standard. This might be a surprising step, but it's important. Grieve the version of yourself you thought necessary to become worthy. Grieve the expectations you felt crushed by. Grieve the times you betrayed yourself trying to gain approval. Grieve the exhaustion of performing worthiness instead of feeling it. You don't need to carry that weight anymore. You get to let it go.

Reclaiming your worth is a process. Sometimes it's messy, sometimes it's slow and that is okay. Every small step is progress.

Now let's redefine what worth means to you. If worth isn't based on your looks, your job, your relationship status, or how many people like you on social media… then what is it based on?

I eventually realized that my worth is intrinsic. It is something I was born with—something that was never up for debate.

Try defining it in a way that empowers you.

For example:

- My worth is not up for negotiation.
- I am valuable simply because I exist.
- Nothing and no one can take away my enough-ness.

Say it again and again, until your body starts to believe it.

Because the truth is—you were always enough. You just learned to forget.

Now, get specific. What beliefs are you holding that keep you feeling unworthy?

Maybe it's:

- If I fail, I'm a failure.
- If I speak up, people will reject me.
- I have to look perfect to be loved.
- Write them down. Don't judge them—just get them out.

Then, rewrite them like this:

- Failure is how I grow. I can fail and still be worthy.
- I can speak my truth and still be loved.
- My appearance doesn't determine my value.

If your brain resists, try creating a "bridge" belief:

- I'm learning to believe I'm enough.
- It's becoming easier to accept my worth.

Keep repeating them. Write them on mirrors. Speak them out loud. Anchor them into your nervous system with time and consistency.

I once had a client who sat across from me, eyes down, fingers twisting anxiously in their lap. After a long pause, they finally whispered, "I hate myself." They told me they had tried all the affirmations people online recommended. They would stand in front of the mirror, stare at their own reflection, and force the words, "I love you" or "You're beautiful." But every time, before the sentence even fully left their lips, a voice in their mind would cut in and snigger "No you're not."

It wasn't that they didn't want to believe differently. Their nervous system simply wasn't ready to leap from self-hatred to self-love in one jump.

So we started where they actually were. I asked them to try something much smaller, something their brain wouldn't immediately reject. Instead of "I love you," they practiced saying, "I'm okay," or even,

"I'm doing fine." The first time they tried it, their shoulders dropped just a little, like their body finally had room to breathe.

It was a tiny bridge almost imperceptible from the outside but it changed everything. With each day, that small, believable statement softened the grip of self-hate. And slowly, the voice that once sneered back began to quiet. From "I'm okay," we eventually built our way to, "I'm worthy of kindness," and then, "I'm learning to like who I am."

It wasn't about forcing love, it was about creating a path toward it. Creating the bridge beliefs, the softened thoughts, building until we believe that we are enough.

If you believed you were already enough right now, as you are, how would you treat yourself? What would your daily actions look like?

My daily actions started to change when I felt like I was enough. They started off quietly and looked like this:

- Picking up the phone and making that call I was scared to make.
- Finally making the doctor and dentist appointments I had been putting off.
- Saying "NO" without the monoglue to go with it.
- Resting without apologizing for it.
- Speaking up in meetings or group settings, even when my voice would shake.
- Asking for help when I needed it.

And then the bigger shifts came:

- Raising my prices even when fear told me not to.
- Launching before I felt ready.

- Calling myself a leader instead of waiting for permission.

- Saying yes to opportunities that once felt "too big" for me.

I remember the first time I raised my rate and sent the email anyway, hands shaking. It was the moment I chose to act as if I was already enough. And something in me changed forever.

These may seem small, but they are powerful. They teach our brains a new rule: I am allowed to take up space exactly how I am.

Would you:

- Feed your body with love and care?

- Set boundaries without guilt?

- Rest without needing to earn it.

- Say no when something doesn't feel aligned?

- Choose relationships that nourish, not deplete you?

- Speak your truth even when your voice shakes?

- Trust your message enough to share it with the world?

You are not fixing yourself; you are rewriting the outdated rules you've been living by.

Here's the secret: you don't have to feel worthy before you start acting like you are.

In fact, acting like you're enough is one of the fastest ways to retrain your brain to believe it's true.

Here's what I want you to know:

You were never broken. You were never too much. You were never not enough.

That voice in your head that tells you otherwise. It's not you.

It's an old belief that you've simply outgrown.

You get to choose something different now.

You get to return to yourself—to that grounded, whole, worthy version of you that's always been there, just waiting to be remembered.

And just like any belief, worthiness is a practice.

So, start today.

Start small.

Start by saying out loud:

"I am enough."

Even if you don't believe it yet. Say it anyway. And then keep showing up like it's true.

Because it is.

You're not broken—you're becoming.

Exercise:

- Can you remember the first time you felt like you weren't "enough"?
  What happened, and how did it make you feel?
  Who was involved? What were you told—or not told—that left a lasting imprint?

- Think about your "not enough" thoughts. Whose voice do they sound like?
  Was it a parent, teacher, friend, or someone else?

- Now ask yourself: Was that belief even true? What might have been going on in their world when they said those things to you?

- How has believing "I'm not enough" affected your life?
  What experiences have you avoided?
  What relationships did you stay in—or never pursue?

What dreams did you put on hold?

- What do you want to believe instead?
  Write three new, empowering beliefs that affirm your inherent worth.
  Example:
    - I am inherently valuable, just as I am.
    - I don't need to prove my worth—I already possess it.
    - My presence is enough.

  Now write your *new story:*
  "I used to believe ___. Now I choose to believe ___."

- If I truly believed I was already enough, what bold move would I finally make in my work, my leadership, or my purpose starting today?

As you step into this truth—that your worth is inherent and unwavering—consider how it shapes the way you show up, lead, and claim the life you were always meant to live.

Epilogue

Well done. You've made it to the end of this journey, rewriting the rules that have shaped your life. You've questioned old beliefs, faced some harsh truths, and started to carve out a path that feels true to you.

Remember, this isn't just a book to read once and put aside. It's a tool to come back to whenever you need a reminder that you have the power to rewrite your story. Growth isn't a straight line; it's a process that takes time and gentle patience.

If you feel ready to dive deeper or need a little extra support, know that you don't have to do this alone. Whether through coaching, workshops, or group programs, there are ways to keep moving forward, ways to help you step fully into your worth and purpose.

I'd love to walk alongside you on that journey. Reach out when you're ready, and let's keep rewriting those rules together.

The life you want? It's closer than you think.

About the Author

Danielle (Nicci) Lee is the founder of Lovingly Guided, a coaching practice that blends mind, emotion, and energy-based techniques to help clients reconnect with their inner power, rewrite limiting beliefs, and move confidently toward the goals that are ready to unfold in their lives. Through her unique, holistic approach, she supports people in accessing the parts of themselves that are waiting to shine.

In addition to her coaching work, Nicci leads transformative retreats that use nature as a grounding force—helping clients slow down, reconnect with themselves, and experience healing through the land.

When she's not working with clients, you'll likely find her hiking or camping deep in the woods, or traveling to explore a new corner of the world. Conservation is one of her greatest passions, and she is currently developing a nonprofit called Keeping Roots, dedicated to protecting land from development so future generations can enjoy, learn from, and be restored by the natural world.

To find out more about Nicci's work and her coaching offerings, visit: www.lovinglyguided.com and www.keepingroots.org

www.ingramcontent.com/pod-product-compliance
Lightning Source LLC
Chambersburg PA
CBHW060359080526
44583CB00012B/388